How Animals Defend Themselves

Written by Etta Kaner
Illustrated by Pat Stephens

Kids Can Press

To Caitlin — P.S.

 ® Kids Can Read is a registered trademark of Kids Can Press Ltd.

Kids Can Press acknowledges the financial support of the Government of Ontario,
through the Ontario Media Development Corporation's Ontario Book Initiative; the
Ontario Arts Council; the Canada Council for the Arts; and the Government of Canada,
through the BPIDP, for our publishing activity.

Published in Canada by
Kids Can Press Ltd.
29 Birch Avenue
Toronto, ON M4V 1E2

Published in the U.S. by
Kids Can Press Ltd.
2250 Military Road
Tonawanda, NY 14150

www.kidscanpress.com

Adapted by David MacDonald from the book *Animal Defenses*.

Edited by David MacDonald
Designed by Sherill Chapman
Educational consultant: Maureen Skinner Weiner, United Synagogue Day School,
Willowdale, Ontario

Printed and bound in China

The hardcover edition of this book is smyth sewn casebound.
The paperback edition of this book is limp sewn with a drawn-on cover.

CM 06 0 9 8 7 6 5 4 3 2 1
CM PA 06 0 9 8 7 6 5 4 3 2 1

Library and Archives Canada Cataloguing in Publication

Kaner, Etta
    How animals defend themselves / written by Etta Kaner ; illustrated by
Pat Stephens. —Rev. ed.

(Kids Can read)
Based on author's Animal defenses.

ISBN-13: 978-1-55337-904-1 (bound) ISBN-10: 1-55337-904-7 (bound)
ISBN-13: 978-1-55337-905-8 (pbk.) ISBN-10: 1-55337-905-5 (pbk.)

1. Animal defenses—Juvenile literature. 2. Animal weapons—Juvenile
literature. I. Stephens, Pat, 1950– II. Kaner, Etta. Animal defenses. III. Title.
IV. Series: Kids Can read (Toronto, Ont.)

PE1119.K35 2006   j591.47   C2006-900129-4

Kids Can Press is a ℓ☺ⲅⵑS™ Entertainment company

Contents

When danger is near

What do you do when you are afraid? Do you yell for help? Do you hide or run away? Some animals do these things too when they are afraid. But many animals protect themselves from danger in amazing ways.

Look at the bright colors of this blue-ringed octopus.

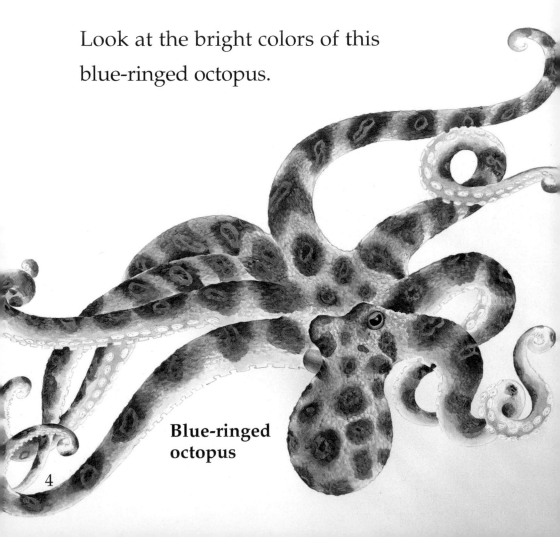

Blue-ringed octopus

Here is what the blue-ringed octopus looks like when danger is near. This octopus can change its colors so it's harder to see it in the ocean.

Read on to find out more about some of the ways animals protect themselves from danger.

Putting on a show

If you were a very small animal, how would you protect yourself from being eaten? Take a look at what these animals do.

Toad

If a snake is near, a toad may puff itself up and stretch out its back legs. This makes it look too big for the snake to swallow.

The citrus swallowtail caterpillar scares away hungry birds by pretending it's a snake. It has a fake red tongue that looks just like the tongue of a snake.

Citrus swallowtail caterpillar

The blue-tongued skink is a kind of lizard. When it's frightened, it sticks out its huge, bright blue tongue. This scares away animals that want to eat it.

Blue-tongued skink

The African cut-throat finch is another animal that pretends to be a snake when danger is near. It can hiss and wriggle its body just like a snake.

African cut-throat finch

Eyed hawkmoth

The eyed hawkmoth looks like a dead leaf when it rests on a branch. But if a hungry bird gets too close, this moth uncovers its back wings. These wings have spots that look like two huge owl eyes. That's enough to scare away any hungry bird!

Can you find me?

When an animal looks a lot like its surroundings, we say it has camouflage. Camouflage makes an animal hard for its enemies to see.

The Australian tawny frogmouth is a bird that sleeps in a tree all day. Its body shape and brown feathers make it look like a broken tree branch.

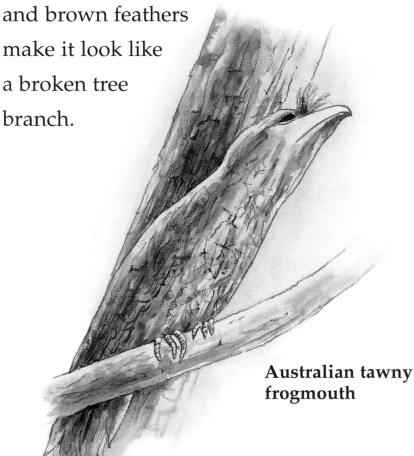

Australian tawny frogmouth

Guess what the decorator crab uses for camouflage. Seaweed! It cuts pieces of seaweed with its claws. Then it sticks the seaweed onto its back. This is a good way to hide from danger.

Decorator crab

The flounder hunts for food at the bottom of the ocean. If it is on a sandy bottom, its skin changes to look like sand. On a rocky bottom, it looks like rocks.

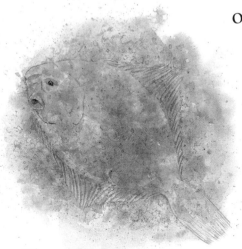

Flounder

The beaver uses branches and mud to build a home in the middle of a pond. Inside, there is a room that is dry and cozy. The only way to get inside is through a secret underwater tunnel. Hungry bears can't get in.

Copycats

Some animals are copycats. They look and act like animals that their enemies don't want to eat.

Birds know that the monarch butterfly is poisonous to eat. The viceroy butterfly looks a lot like the monarch butterfly. So birds stay away from both kinds of butterflies.

Viceroy butterfly

Monarch butterfly

Birds and lizards eat spiders, but they don't touch ants. That's why many spiders try to look like ants. They hold two legs in front of their head to look like an ant's antennae.

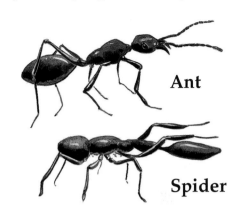

Ant

Spider

Birds don't eat honeybees because they know honeybees can sting. The hoverfly looks enough like a honeybee to fool birds. The hoverfly will even buzz like a bee if a bird is near.

Hoverfly

Honeybee

Are these two snakes twins? Look closely at the stripes and you'll see that they are different. The coral snake is poisonous, but the king snake is not. Animals can't tell the difference between these two snakes, so they stay away from both kinds.

Coral snake

16

King snake

You can't hurt me

Some animals have a hard shell that protects them from being hurt by other animals.

Turtles have a hard shell that protects their body. The three-toed box turtle has a special kind of shell. The bottom part of its shell can fold up, keeping the turtle safe inside.

Box turtle

**Box turtle with
bottom shell folded up**

The three-banded armadillo rolls itself into a ball if an animal tries to attack. The hard shells on the outside of the ball protect the armadillo.

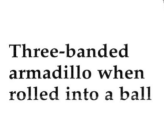

Three-banded armadillo when rolled into a ball

A thick, heavy shell protects the giant clam. Its shell is as long as a bathtub! No animal can break or open the giant clam's shell.

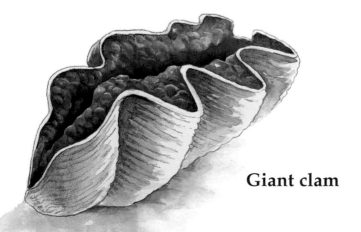

Giant clam

The North American porcupine's body is covered with thousands of sharp quills. If an animal tries to attack, the porcupine swings its tail back and forth. The quills stick into the attacker when it gets hit by the tail.

**Tip of a
porcupine quill**

Warning, stay away!

Some animals have bright colors that send a warning to their enemies — "Stay away! Don't eat me! I'll make you sick!"

The striped skunk has two white stripes down its back. These stripes tell enemies to stay away. If they don't, the skunk sprays them in the face. The spray doesn't just smell bad. It can make an enemy blind for several hours.

Striped skunk

Ladybugs are bright red or yellow, with black. These colors tell birds, spiders and beetles not to eat ladybugs. They taste horrible!

Ladybug

The Oriental fire-bellied toad shows enemies the bright orange on its belly. This is a warning that the toad's skin has a poison that burns.

Oriental fire-bellied toad

These poison-arrow frogs live in rain forests in South America. Their bright colors tell enemies that their skin is poisonous. A bird or snake that tries to eat one of these frogs will spit it out right away.

Let's stick together

Some animals try to stay safe by living in groups. Other animals live with a different kind of animal, and they help each other out. Sticking together is safer than living alone.

Dolphins live in groups. If a hungry shark comes near, the dolphins attack it. They hit the shark all over with their beaks.

Dolphins attacking a shark

Impala

Baboon

Impalas and baboons often travel together.
Impalas are good at hearing and smelling
danger. Baboons are good at seeing danger.
Together, they help each other stay safe
from enemies.

The oxpecker bird lives on the back of the African buffalo. Why? Because it eats insects that live in the buffalo's skin.

If danger comes near, the oxpecker warns the buffalo. It calls out and flaps its wings. If the buffalo doesn't pay attention, the oxpecker pecks the buffalo on the head!

Oxpecker bird

African buffalo

Shrimp

Luther's goby

A little fish called Luther's goby and a blind shrimp are good partners. The shrimp digs a burrow for both to live in.

The goby leads the shrimp out on feeding trips. The shrimp keeps its antennae in touch with the goby's tail. If the goby wiggles its tail, the shrimp knows there is danger.
The two go to hide in their burrow.

Playing tricks

Many animals save their lives by playing tricks on their enemies.

American opossum

The hognose snake and the American opossum both fool enemies by pretending they're dead. The hognose snake even drips blood out of its open mouth!

Hognose snake

If an enemy grabs the tail of a leopard gecko, guess what happens. The tail breaks off — and keeps on wiggling! This surprises the enemy and gives the gecko time to escape.

The gecko's tail will grow back, but it won't be as long or straight as it was before.

Leopard gecko

You can't catch me

Many animals can escape from danger because they're fast. They can quickly run, fly or swim away.

The Australian sugar-glider can't fly like a bird, but it can glide through the air. It sails from one tree to another by stretching out skin flaps on the sides of its body. It steers with its fluffy tail.

Australian sugar-glider